SKINS ON THE EARTH

Skins on the Earth

PRIMUS ST. JOHN

COPPER CANYON PRESS

Port Townsend   1976

Poems in this collection have appeared in the following magazines: *American Poetry Review, Chesepeake Weekly Review, Choice, Concerning Poetry, Copperhead, Dryad, Iowa Review, Northwest Review, Pioneer Log, Poetry Northwest, Poetry Now, Works*
and anthologies:
Poems & Perspectives (Scott-Foresman & Co.), *The Poetry of Black America in the 20th Century* (Harper & Row), *American Poetry in 1976* (Bobbs-Merrill), and *Zero Makes Me Hungry* (Scott-Foresman).

SPECIAL THANKS TO:

Centrum Foundation, Fort Worden State Park, Port Townsend, Washington, where Copper Canyon is Press-in-Residence; and, for a grant which in part made possible publication of this book, the National Endowment for the Arts, a federal agency.

Copyright © 1976 by Primus St. John
All rights reserved
Printed in the United States of America
Library of Congress Cataloging in Publication Data
St. John, Primus, 1939-
   Skins on the earth.
    I. Title.
PS3569.A454S55   811'.5'4   75-14652
ISBN 0-914742-07-8

CONTENTS

I

9 All the Way Home
11 Benign Neglect
12 Our Lady of Congress
14 American Roots
16 Elephant Rock
19 If You Find This, Send for Me
21 Oluranti
22 A Splendid Thing Growing
24 He Imagined the Gorgeous Pattern of the New Skin and Settled for America
26 Strike One, Strike Two: A Savage Song
27 The Holy Ghost will not Materialize
28 Love and the Evil that is Victorious
29 The Loyal Opposition

II

33 The Violence of Pronoun
35 Water Can Only Wrap Me, But Life Must Hold Me
36 Eloma
37 Esom
38 For These Conditions there is No Abortion
40 My Main Squeeze
41 Laborer
42 Indeed
43 Bedding Down
44 The Carpenter
46 After the Truckers Restaurant
47 Late Assignment
49 Two Voices from Hester St. (1904)

III

53 Riding the Wolver Hollow Road
55 Tyson's Corner
56 Constellations
58 Southern Comfort
60 Lynching and Burning
61 Bussing: Autumn as Fiction
62 Looking at a Bus Stop
63 Into the Open Heart
64 Survival
65 The Dark God of Roses

IV

71 Delivery
72 The Morning Star
73 The Fountain
74 Field
76 Biological Light
78 Studying
79 Westward Expansion
80 Poem for my Notebook, Across Winter
81 A Lasting Peace
82 Waking

"Though we do not believe it yet the interior life is a real life, and the intangible dreams of people have a tangible effect on the world."

ALL THE WAY HOME

The lamps hung like a lynching
In my town.
It was a dark town.
In a dark town,
Light is a ragged scar.
Fright begs that ragged scar.
It begs doorways.

I love that town.
From its lean men
I learned
Emotion;
And how to hold that fine edge,
That makes us
        people . . .

Mrs. Blackwell's
Sold her house.
Since her husband revolved his head,
She wears bright hats
That speak to people.

B.J.'s doing time.
His children betray that time,
By the breathing it takes
To dream through windows.
Mary Lee dreams him letters;
She dreams by heart . . .

Now I feel a new scar.
I've left home
And leaned so far,
I'm almost zero.
And though it's lonely
Whatever knowing is;
It strings a long fine wire.
At night I lie awake
And listen to that wire—

All the way home.

BENIGN NEGLECT/
WEST POINT, MISSISSIPPI, 1970

Suppose you were dreaming about your family,
And when you woke up
You found a man named Sonny Stanley
Had just shot you (5 times),
Or justice
Looked just like the color your blood was running—
Running wild in the world—
But the world wouldn't see.
Then
You read, somewhere
(I think it's the papers)
If it's a problem, Boy,
We don't have one here
We don't ask a man to die
Like groceries babbling froth to flies.
But bleeding,
You watch your neighbors
Write away to their windows to
Hide! Hide!
    "He's not there. He's not there."
The last sentence?
The last sentence is your *Father*—
One of the windows . . .
    "He's not there. He's not there."

        Goodbye, Johnny.

OUR LADY OF CONGRESS

The opposition likes dry poems—
No storms
That are holding hands
The same way
It begins to rain
When we suspect our lives.
The answer to everything
Is a just peace
(So we elected him president),
Or better umbrellas
That are not afraid.
It is an aesthetic form
History has taken,
To adjust time to a sea shell
When strong water comes.
So we go back on our lives.
Reliving all of our curves when we were worms.
Caution, inside
Never learns
No poem is listening to our
Lives—
This way,
Not even the earth.

Justice is in stones
With thirst.
Large storms live on weight
And look our way
When the seals are broken.
Water is success
Whispered to stone like slime.
What we are behind our faces
Is a crack that's leaking,
A yell that's lost its body in a shell.
There are no more words
For old yankee faces like ours,
But the luck we have left.

AMERICAN ROOTS: MORAL ASSOCIATIONS

1
Kinship:
Is embarassing the wind,
Like dead black boys,
Falling down from the trees,
Then down stream—
On their knees,
Blood like,
Like a rich nation.

2
Metaphor:
Becomes humiliating,
And clean,
Ticking like a ripe machine.
Do not
Bend,
Fold,
Or mutilate me—
This is your future speaking.

3
The air smells so metaphysical
We have accused it—
Of smog,
And lost manhood,
Then all ritual.

4
Whoever wrote:
A view is a mountain speaking
But left the introduction
For the snow,
And accused silence
Of its soul.

5
The whole nation:
Is a stanza of blackness,
A huge white whale,
Faith in space
(Like the newspapers),
And the quiet insistence
We have peace,
And it's your world, brother.

ELEPHANT ROCK

    We take place in what we believe.
    I've memorized that
                    Because
    It's life
         And that
    Invisible—
    If you're thinking in the dark.

    Take the line we drew
    Around   Elephant Rock,
         A beginning
    That could happen
         Any day
    You put your thumb
             Down
    That long block
    And saw all neighbors
         As trees.

    On our side
    We kept these
         Possibilities;
            1.   Mount up now
            2.   You're ten
            3.   This country is your trail too

We began to see
Near this rock
        What did not look right
In our books,
        That presence
Was enough
And
Anyone who worked
Should be free
        To meet himself—
Sometime.

We called it
Cowboys and Indians
           Or
The girls should stay home
It's safe that way.
But every day this
        Mythology
Grew
We'd lose time
And we'd lose.

One day, Jerry said
Believe—
        Go ahead
          Believe.

We tried—
To keep the thin trails,
Old trees,
But there's something wrong
        with America—
If you're Black

Believe—
>	Go ahead,
>		Believe.

These three were the most creative:
>	*Breno Jones*
>	he left five kids,
>	and a thin, incredible
>	wife.
>	*Duke*
>	he was never lucky,
>	he just died
>		&
>	*Jerry* too,
>		O.D.'d
At the feet of Elephant Rock . . .

And because even this is not enough,
>	Something else,
Over their heads
That still takes place
>	in America.
Old walls
>	&
Tall rocks
With that sign
I could never understand —

>	JESUS SAVES

IF YOU FIND THIS, SEND FOR ME

Brigham's Legacy

Coming through the pass
The men have stuck their eyes out.
Faith and loneliness, Lord
Is this your word.
It has grown things that hurt
And help control the wagons
'til they creak like gossip
Around our thighs.
Every night is worse.
The horses are dumb and patient
Only their tails work . . .
Or is even this   imagination.
They have entered my thoughts, too much,
And become culture.

Deseret

The only place
For a citizen is religion.
They like it around here —
the way God's snow
Scrubs everything white
Is fierce revelation . . .

Everything —
Even the blood in their veins
Is no oversight . . .

This is the type of country
Where you know it — or you don't.

The Angel Mormon

Books are lost.
So men's words come back:
> Stones...

Worse than that—
The ways they believe them.
Calling out:
> *Ghost*
> *Angels*
> *All the lost tribes* . . .

(Inspiring.)
In New England or New York
Joseph Smith touched himself,
It is written
Such quiet pain involves us all—
Or the Angel.

The Black Mormon

My name is Genesis:
And irony shapes this world
And this world's light.
It is alright—
> Believe me.

Since the first breath
Troubled everything,
I have known
Everything is everything
(And suffered it)
This is my curse . . .

If you find this, send for me.

OLURANTI

Planting roses,
History comes back.
Moses was a strange man.
He pitched tents,
And saved rocks
Like God told him to grow old.
Now that the mud is shared,
By both my knees
I look out for that country.
A river comes from the north.
What happened out there
Took 40 years;
Most of us slept,
Couldn't hear,
Blamed the rain
For the threatening edges.
Night after night
Most of us walked,
Talked in our sleep...
There were no roses,
But he waited.

A SPLENDID THING GROWING

Chair:
It is the name of me.
The ending of my arms
And the ending of my legs
Mean nothing.
I cannot creak enough.

Dish:
It is the emptiness.
I am going to breath
Over the edge,
And feel—
Louder.

Vase:
And water are righteousness.
So flowers are given,
So dance,
And wind
        within us.

Cup:
It is the round place.
So is intention.
So is our drinking.

Godliness:
That is knife.
Given decision.
Given harshness
        like cut.

Table:
Be with me
On this earth.
It is set with our flesh.

Come closer:
Like carpet
And trust.
Dust in us
Everything woven.

Drapes:
They are disturbances,
And thinking.
Flapping makes no sense,
But storms.

Doom:
It is always left.
At night,
It is a splendid thing growing.
It shows us nothing.

Oh Nouns ! Forgive us.

HE IMAGINED THE GORGEOUS PATTERN OF THE NEW SKIN AND SETTLED FOR AMERICA

The quiet which is my wife endures:
I have hurt nothing, unless we have touched.

It is the indicative mood,   after desire
The Deerslayer

Now middle aged
Has become lonesome and white again

Rising up out of the continent
That is Chingachgook

Red skinned, red eyed morning light
The myth that has happened to the democratic.

That black man over there:
Slaughtered in the hills of my wife . . .

Imagination,
Black and breathing.

I   am slaughtered in his wife,
It has happened to meaning.

Fit to be Satan — now:
Cooper, Hawthorne, Melville's

I wear my dark skinned hat —
Irreconcilable

In the final phase. Satanic,
It seems to fit me right.

To walk away alone
Into the sunset of our bleeding children.

STRIKE ONE, STRIKE TWO: A SAVAGE SONG

I am as safe as I can
Slide into the softball game (Sunday).
Nothing happens to men
But the phallic deed.
The tight hands around the bat
Like a negative
(Mother, print that).

Beer is savage, at last, I am delivered.
In a year's fat, or two,
I will be pregnant enough
To go home.

Over the years,
I have elected the men
Unpassionate enough
To understand that.
Lately, out of sheer myth
They're fucking it up.

You've got to pitch the ball in
Like a gun rack
Floating across an imperfect pick up.
Brush the coloreds back from my wife
(I mean life).
Darling, I look forward to seeing you (Sunday).
The metaphor is *put it here babe*
                    put it here babe
                    put it here.

THE HOLY GHOST WILL NOT MATERIALIZE

This poem:
Fire of thighs, the breathing wind
And me big pioneer
Is uncouth.
I want to sleep at night, mix the metaphors,
Stark dumb
My impression of the unconscious.

The loveliest woman
Is cruel iron.
I beat the forge of her soul
Pregnant, with war.

The trouble with Time
Is it's organic.
It means she bleeds,
Blood ruins everything.
Blood

Blood,
I'm going to war.
Backwoodsman alone in paradise
>*in the name of the father,*
>*the son, and the ghost.*

LOVE AND THE EVIL THAT IS VICTORIOUS

    I've had it:

    She is no cut and dry solution.
    Love is unorthodox . . .

    It always goes this way:

    First, the western jay stays quiet
    And we move.
    She breaks me down to heart
    (the beat is uncouth)
    Then, pure spring, I flow against my will
    (*Now*, do you know why I dislike you?)

    We begin in the world with nothing:

    A germ called *money* blooms,
    I am its pregnant fool.

    In terms of the world,
    She keeps looking at me
    Like my body doesn't even understand

    Democracy.

THE LOYAL OPPOSITION

Now, in this third world
The butcher tries to cut the light
While it plays (*He is a weird dude*)
Because it is just a witness
like my wife.
It thighs away
Into those green hills
And bears this dark child
That is accurate with smiles.

Night:
At a time like this,
We can always see
This child's
One eyed dream take shape,
Or impeach
What we have discovered about (this) child's dream.
We can deal with ourselves,
Like Hawthorne—
Gothic, though the letter is red
In our soul like a bleeding rose.

Maybe, tonight, reader,
When darkness is just
An immense poem
Longing for a simpler past,
We will just resign.
I don't think so
It is too late.

"This is the meal equally set, this is the meat for natural hunger"

THE VIOLENCE OF PRONOUN

1
Loving came her way,
        vicious.
It rose up,
From the earth,
And made her father's hand,
Around her throat,
A bird of prey,
And carried her away—
        In mind,
Like a limp patient.
He was not drunk.
It is worse.
In this world,
We cannot feel ...

2
In my sociology class —
        For understanding
Black folks —
They tried to understand
Our homes —
        Like buckshot.
What we have done,
        To love
Is unforgivable.
They took out rakes,
And treated us like dirt.
It was so perfect
They asked for grades.

3
Leaving people out of this—
I can forgive.
I married her, anyway
And in the church,
When I unfolded her hand,
                I saw

In her palm
The way she would die . . .
Leaping out of democracy,
Through some weird window,
                white
With the wilderness of God—
            1965 Memorial Day.
And I went on, crazy
        at first,
And crazy even now
For being so unmilitant . . .

4
What I told that class,
(You know) they said it hurt.
"It is our innocence
That makes us vicious."

WATER CAN ONLY WRAP ME, BUT LIFE MUST HOLD ME

A black man, from Oklahoma,
Married moisture.
Her name was Ruth.

Whenever he talked a stone
Cracked for water,
But not for doom.

Over the years she has become
Sweeter, listening
Like a horned toad;
At nights,
Wearing only her own
Horned toad clothes—
But breathing
As strong as they fit her.

It has been years . . .
Love and exposure have become poem.

ELOMA

We have not built the train
Here, our tracks are our own steel
Storms.

At night, we build the right fire
And watch the smoke—
That emphasizes things.

He ordered me like a book
He has read aloud:
Unresolved, without refuge.

I came to him for miles
On the hips of wagon
To be *unowned*.

Ever since the days of cotton
I have been unredeemed.
Whitmanesque as the bells
I go to my wanderer

Possessed.

ESOM

Many things in one are black.
I want to emphasize the soil—
Black
Irony against unnamed pain.

I have dreamed of a wilderness
Called Woman,
Her black knees with ash
Part soil, part rain
Where I can find the root of things

Like Name:
Full and rounded and unredeemed.

We will call our way seed
Like children again

Our impact on the smoke.

FOR THESE CONDITIONS THERE IS NO ABORTION

1

They say the tongue is only *Praexis*.
It is only a surge forward
Between Spring and God.
Months later,
God is gone. Our spring is upon us.
We learn the names for children,
They don't want us or our child.
We are just sophomores and curses.
Like Aristotle
I believe plot after plot
Means something.
It is a formula evening:
The sun is red
Night is someone beyond blue
Her belly is living and dying
And we don't sit close anymore —
Even in the lunchroom.
Her eyes are smooth stones, falling
I am a man,
Therefore I am falling.
She says today she has learned a word
For folks like us,
I am about to say sorry
She says *pathos* . . .

2
Martha's story is not so simple (*yes*).
She is older and freer
Like her lover is gone (*yes*)
And she is poor, (*yes*),
Poor Martha:
With her belly in her hands
With a man who is anything but Jesus.
Poor Martha:
With blood and misunderstanding
Tragedy is opening for all her roses.

Lord, legalize this:
Our bloom and decay.

Martha is something in common with rope
On fire.
Her womb should give her pleasure,
Not *hangers* and *quinine* and *soda*.

MY MAIN SQUEEZE

For a raw season,
I bite the rhythm of her blood
Listening silence,
Throbbing, for more flesh.

Each of her lips
Are the little birds
That miss their wings
By too much breathing.

Later,
Cripples near sleep
Our red eyes
Stay
Close in the dark,
Rolling
In those old hills
Of our severe sweat.

Legends of this
Smolder in our campfire
And the night grows as quiet
As an old African chief
Our stunned fingers know well.

LABORER

I work for what I get.
I get words.
I take them out the rent—
In hate.

I come home late,
It does not work.
She listens to me
Like germs.

I am so drunk,
My shoes are cracked.
She will go away
Through the openings
Taking nothing.

Of all the colors,
I know,
Black is the most truthful
To her children.

INDEED

for Joanne

   I married a girl in the summer who slept on the beach.
I married her feet, sandlike, and gathered her limbs.
These dreams,
Flesh, are so remote, about 500,000 years in darkness.
A loss crows would seek repose in the shudders of the
                                                    earth
And become dancers.
   Each day I am amazed at stones. They hear me. They
                                                    break
Into our children, are ruined again and again to grow,
                                                      but
Baked bread crumbs — resounding their lives like brooms
   Indeed I think I have made a move—from thighs,
To silence, to you. It is a good one.

BEDDING DOWN

The redness of the apples
Cannot see,
I understand
In the night black air
The smells of no fear—
Breathing,
Just the crackling
Of bent limbs in hidden places.
I smell the reasons,
They are all sweet,
Pitch black,
Unknown.
I go down on my hands,
And on my knees,
And shed my skin—
For health,
And spend the night.

THE CARPENTER

1

I look at my hands
In a dark hour.
They are my wife,
Another life,
Faunal,
Explicitly made.
I compare responsibility
To journey
They are pitch black
Whirling in the outside world
Left behind like a native—
Possessed.

2

We are older:
Toil is our long way
Back home.
It works.
Causes the space to beat
Like a heart.
It is a part of the poem
That appears
And appears on its own.
It goes on
On its own,
Mystical as evil
But, it is called freedom.

3

I'm sorry:
I was telling you about my hands.
How well we are married.
It follows,
I recognize all truth
As some part of ten.
Spirit is my thumb,
Passionately.
Without thumb
I would be nothing.
I have met some who believe in reason.
They have had too much wine,
Confess cause and effect
It has been painful.

4

I told you it is unreasonable:
I guess I should say here,
I am your carpenter.
Ethically, dark wood
Is my life.
I could show you my story better,
Sanding,
Then when I speak
You would hear
>   *Africa*
>   *Africa*
One more thing, my love.
I have discovered in this dark wood
A skill you have called our loneliness.
I sand it down for you
Until our bodies fall off.

AFTER THE TRUCKERS RESTAURANT

Men look at curves in the dark,
With both their eyes.
Any line that is a turned mouth—
In the sides of a mountain,
          truckers believe,
You can turn to a nerve
In that mouth
That screams so no one hears it.

In sleeping,
My woman breathes a sign
On the window,
About zeros blinking.
          (She's trusting.)
To touch that trust
I trace my hand
Where all zeros come from.

I am a man as black
As the back of every curve,
That awaits me.
My headlights are on,
          (highbeam, if that can help),
And I hear voices
Coming from all of the spots
I will never see
          Off the roads in the dark.

Whatever I will do tonight,
That's coming too.
I can hear it.
She can hear it (sleeping).

LATE ASSIGNMENT

All the light in the world
            is a dream—
the world is keeping—
to keep
        the world
                alive.
        God!
the books I have to read;
and the thoughts
            I have to keep—
or fail.

In the classics,
there is a faith:
        If you are lucky
                to be
made with the finer stones,
    you are classified enough,
and should
        go on . . .

        Body,
I know it's too late;
            but
we have come too far . . .
and these books
        and the flights they keep
                are wrong.

The blood has a statement
    to make,
that goes round
        and round
the bones;
and when we're through,
it says the bones
       were wrong.

In a million
      years,
there will be a scar
    in our place;
not enough for the world
to remember.
But if there is luck,
    something will come
             along—
                and wait;
perhaps with a hand—
    or something
        more.

The wind will come.
And whatever light is—
    will come;
but not remember . . .

My woman is across the room;
              asleep.
Right now,
    there is a fine rain
          looking
for the center
        of the earth.

TWO VOICES FROM HESTER ST. (1904)

1

This morning
In the warm air,
I paint the sheets out
My window
That beat my life
Until I am mad
In the dry hand
Of clothes pins.

I am a psalm
In this new land—
Like a barn filled with wheat
And flies.
My white skinned music
Grins, lost, in the air.

2

I see her hair
I see her hair—
Sing.
The black birds are wild.
They declare
They declare
The common things.
The famine and the grin,
In the eyes of the poor.
Their wings are unreachable
Strands,
They tear my life
Raw
Wife this morning,
Controlled like the vegetables
Down stairs
Down in the bins
Down in the bins
Speechless
And religious with the crowds
Is my love for her.
If I could take the crows
Of her hair
With me
Down the stairway
And hang them in front of me
For the darkness,
Something we have suspected
Would rise up in our hands
Would say
  Abraham
  Abraham

III

"And there was this adult pain
Down deep in the soul
Because of which was laughter"

RIDING THE WOLVER HOLLOW ROAD

To find in my flesh
The smell of fresh bread
Rising from the window,
Rex, running down the yard
Beside my arm,
That is what I dreamed.
But I'm not young now,
And the Wolver Hollow road
Goes on—
Wearing in the windshield,
My life
Dry
Asking for water,
Like the cripple child
You insist I call
A pine tree.

Oh yes I'm a madman mother,
Running my life away
To quench a storm,
And all this talk of God—
And surely his mercy!—
Eats away my lining,
With its picture
Of large dreams,
Crushed in this latest sociological plan
For making your son John
A constructive
And highly effective man.

I am tired of the smell
Of prosperity
Fencing in the land;
Of an old bitch,
Unfit to dream
Wearing out her children
With special schools
And special rules.
I want the woodchuck
Rambling home,
Full the smell of acorns in his skin.
To see the ant
Hurrying for his doorstep
Faster than my fastest dream.
That is what I want mother:

To smile,
And jumping up
Defy gravity,
Rolling west,
On this two lane road,
Separated by a white line
From the oncoming traffic,
Despite its winding,
Going east.

TYSON'S CORNER

We were as tough as our glasses.
Wires,
That bend around packages
As tight as questions;
Sometimes,
Too tight like mistakes we've made.

When the cop said:
All that blood, son, is your father,
To a boy just like us;
We looked over our rims for some mistake—
Any mistake,
But the barber didn't make one.
He'd cut that time
As deep as true feelings.

Ronnie and I were thin then . . .
And sure.
Dracula, would never come for us . . .
Not us.
But we made a promise:
    For this blood
    For the whole world's
We made a promise.

CONSTELLATIONS

Night time.
'fore I go to bed,
Grandma say,
Put the water to your head...
Shoo
Grandma ole
She say what she want to
And folks say it all true.
What is true...
Face all wet
'fore I sleep.
But,
Later on
In my bed
By the window,
I tug the quilt
Tight as the lights out...
Shoo
I look 'cross all the roofs I know
Feeling brave,
But the roofs ain't brave.
Farther out I see the bear—
Bear don't scare me—
Dip down
Deep in the blue water
O' grandma's God.
I hear grandma snore, loud
But the bear he don't move.
He stopped there
With the water on his face.

His child near by,
By a million years too...
Shoo
What going on that they do
What grandma say.
Everybody know
Grandma ole.

SOUTHERN COMFORT: A GENTLEMAN

1

Evenings
The sky turns blood,
And air
Begins to bleed
Down the broken sticks
Of the bent roads.
The world is soft,
Coming off,
Don't say a word.
It's complicated—
The ways of the roofs of the shacks
Are all dull money,
And hope—
To collect.
There are children,
There is history,
There are words,
There is life
And there is the hungry moon.

2
I own this farm:
So well,
The tin lights are swinging
In my soul.
If this metaphor is not lonely,
Sell all my black feet
And their children's children,
Sell history,
Then the religion that grows white
In the fields,
Sell that
Goddamned self-sufficiency—
Until it's quiet here
And I'm free.

3
Customs come back
To the window.
I'm drunk,
Or soft
Like the chains on the roots
Of cotton.
For life I smoke
And make ghost.
Singing on Sunday
Those black songs
Are flying again,
Their wings beat like more men
Are coming,
Or lost.

LYNCHING AND BURNING

    Men lean toward the wood.
    Hoods   crease
    Until they find people
    Where there used to be hoods.
    Instead of a story,
    The whole thing becomes a scream
        then time, place, far,
        late in the country,
        alone,
        an old man's farm.
    Children we used to call charcoal,
    Now they smell that way—deliberately,
    And the moon stares at smoke like iced tea.

    Daughter,
        Once there was a place we called the earth.
        People lived there. Now we live there . . .

BUSSING: AUTUMN AS FICTION

1
In this neighborhood,
The cornerstones are hair.
I am a strange boy;
The windows do not want me,
And the houses are nails—
Held together, in wood.
It is Nineteen Hundred and Seventy One—

American Gothic

2
The little black girl
Rubs the silence.
It is cold in this room
Like all the flowers
That grow in this season
But won't cry.

3
The bus is breathing.
Home !
Home !
Yellow has come to eat children,
Digest children—
Home!

LOOKING AT A BUS STOP

Water is just a five letter word.
Because it is wet,
Late: thoughts let us men
Wait, impatiently,
As orange as the bus is
Not on time.
Down the street,
The trees are making mistakes
About something.
Their words are only the leaves
That are left, skeptical
As bones
And the same color
That autumn hurts.

INTO THE OPEN HEART

The way the willow tree
Hangs in the fog:
Arms down,
Arms down so far
I know they are personal reasons
That have turned and become—
Like old dog's tails,
But I can't figure suffering out . . .
Finally, who can
Think that far—
Into the open heart.
What is there about love and infirmity
That makes things happen.

SURVIVAL

      Where is my father?
      Black got the man,
      Deep inside,
      All by himself.

THE DARK GOD OF ROSES

It rains like this
    every day
And we only call it pain.
It is so invisible
It knows our name
    to the bone,
And wet
We've let the dirty street
Beat out this story.

Warren
If I see your father, first
I'll kill-em.
That's what gone means.
    So what
Grandma told me,
Don't act like God,
He's not that blind.

Blind
That's poverty, bad teeth
And peanut butter sandwiches,
They look like your *momma*
Your burnt out *momma*.

Dark
Like a church inside,
Bourboned
In stained glass
On this earth
On her knees
Like all of us, here . . .

A garden of blood
In new Caanen.
Don't be afraid of it all.
You came and you go
Like a rose.
Oh Grandma
She's only a rose.

I know this rose
Made up her mind, now,
And paid for it,
And paid
So much.
Her bones were as silly
As old railroad track.

Oh Grandma!
The images in this rose.
American
And kitchened,
The way Miss Anne said
She never loved it,
Lately
And it is still a mistake
Deeper than her face.

Well,
It's too late.
Warren!
Your *momma* should be President
And unpaid,
And I'll be damned if she can't
Survive
Baby after baby
With the vengeance of welfare.

Not innocent
Not rich
Not free
Not even with her consciousness raised.

"Turn to the center given and do the best you can"

DELIVERY

All awakenings are sharp:
We have broken away,
And when we lay, outcast,
In our new sleep;
It is like the forest.
We can tell,
We have power.
We have the power of our arms, out,
Over the color of our faces.
The landscape, dark,
A republic of thought.

Right now, our arms are out.
We are young
The things they say,
My God!
In our world they are so black
I would recognize them anyway
They are unpleasant enough
To be our negroes.

And I for one confess
And if I sleep well,
As well as we have to be a Nation,
This poem will last forever.

THE MORNING STAR

Rumors open up
Way down the road.
The leaves include everything
Like they're really smart.
Then there is an old car
That runs on real red smoke
When the porch goes *thump*.

Mr. Anderson delivers the Stars
And never has to say anything.

I vote for Mr. Anderson.

THE FOUNTAIN

There is always some fountain
Where the water that's really pouring—
Is our lives.
When I hear it,
I believe in all of the storms—
Where it came from.
Then I make believe
I am one of those mossed backed prophets
That sticks on stone and waits
For everything—quietly.

"We are all pouring toward the same conviction,"
I hear the fountain say,
"But we believe that, separately,"
So I believe it all—
The whole thing's that mindless,
And today is spring.

FIELD

1

The day needs curtains
So the wind uses butterflies,
But there is no one at home
Like the buttercups,
Who come by their yellow decisions
Again and again
To see you.
Evenly around, the temporary edges
Of apples, like children,
My face becomes accustomed to sudden
Endings of rain;
And I slosh again,
Descending, gracefully,
Looking for worms.

2

At social gatherings,
Worms eat apples and read my books.
If they had feet,
I could call them Charlemagne.
Sunlight conquers the grass
By flashing blades,
Once in awhile
I crack a twig—
To prove the shade is suffering.

Charlemagne, who needs you !

3
A river is a mouth.
When it screams,
Fish disappear.
I touch my reel, uncomfortably,
And call the tension, Brother.
Huddlers in the deep
Meet the same broken dreams
On land we call unreasonable.
I go back to read,
And repeat,

Charlemagne, who needs you !

   4
Lock the gate, like you're the owner
Behind the pasture;
Take your time reaching the car,
Use your life,
Understand the fish you've caught,
The worms they ate who read,
And poor Charlemagne.

BIOLOGICAL LIGHT

We live here to eat;
Things stare at us.
Those things eat.
We call all of this hunger
The world.
Why ?
Because we live here . . .

All over the world
Morning light is still happening
Like God.
It is so hard to tell
Who eats the plants first—
    Insect or crepuscular.

The wind feels the smallest birds
It's got.
If that is what we are,
It's not a lot—
Here comes the fox.

Noon: circles logically like the hawk.
God moves the rim around
Until the fox is in.
Now the fox is the hawk
And all the small things he ate
Believe him . . .

I have come here late;
The deer look like they have gone,
But thorns remind me
More is going on.

Gradually, memory sets the table back,
I have come from,
Across the water, as far back,
As I can know.
Friends there have eaten me;
Now I stand here, that torn by hate
As I myself have eaten them.

Late; the owls say *whooo*
For what more will surely come.
Finally, I am older—
But not enough—
Surrounded by what I know
Is falling back toward the grass
More like luck than hope...

I am just lying here
Thinking this in my sleep—
How cold it is outside.
If we were fish where it is very dark
It would all be so easy
Light would come from the dead things that we eat.

STUDYING

American Lit. is beside you—
Keep up—
By a small cup
And smaller words . . .
It is night—
By tin cans of light
About the river
You are faithful . . .
But where does it go,
Which soul,
Slanted roof,
Bolted door . . .
There is absolutely nothing here,
But the very late birds,
And what you are.

WESTWARD EXPANSION

When they built these towns
Between the logs
The Indians stared.
Everyone knows, why, now.

The uprisings have come and gone.
Everyone looks backwards—
Through the snow,
The answer is cold,
They were merciless.
Everyone knows, why, now.

If some hand, a claw, still scratching,
Remains,
It is in an empty hole.
A medicine man said it—long ago:
The God of this is awful.
Everyone knows, why, now.

        The truth
In country like this
Where you drive the roads
Through winter, slowly
In chains,
Is the savage painted just like passion
Was only loneliness...

Listen...

Hear how toothless it was
When Natty Bumppo died.

A POEM TO MY NOTEBOOK, ACROSS WINTER

        The flock of birds takes shape
              If there is faith...
in the world, today
It is scattered, and the space
is lonely,
high up there, and cold.
           The leader,
I am afraid of these birds
Thumps for things...
this is hope   or
it is not a poem.
The tradition keeps flapping,
      wrong,
across the sun,
obtrusively like an author's intervention.
It's incomplete, rich experience,
but the best tip yet is dipping,
then diving, deep to the left...
           I hope

A LASTING PEACE

A Lizard is still living:
Passage ways torn out,
Blood in the mouth,
Around his own bone
Desert.
In some deep way of life,
Hung out in the sun,
His lungs stay white...
Beyond pathos.

I have stopped walking.

When pain is red,
It is the aftermath of war...
And more war, to end war.
It is such a great condition,
That it bleeds us—
From the sun   more
& more—every day.
Those who no longer feel this
Have not survived.

WAKING

1
Neither is the case:
Good or *Morning*.

Actually it is the color of the air,
Red as the law.
The green crimed trees
Not moving
Condemned by the birds.

2
If I were judge
I'd do this — *seek patience.*

What happens to the things we love . . .
They are here
They are not here
Like insects, they shame us
With their wings.

The clear meaning of them.
The nascent wisp.

3
I go right out the door:

If I am allowed free play, reader
The light on my skin will be moved
Like a young horse.
I will not notice the froth
In her mouth from patience —

I will not notice.

   4
At the end of the lawn,
One day.
In one of those stories,
One day,
About these bright flowers
The wood chips, soaked
                acid
and absolute—
Who knows how much time we could have
But just in case

I Love You.

Designed & printed by Sam Hamill and Tree Swenson. 1000 copies have been sewn into paper wrappers, and 40 copies, signed by the poet, have been bound in cloth over boards and slipcased. Binding is by Lincoln & Allen, Portland. The type is 12 & 14 pt. Goudy Light, and was set by hand. The paper is Curtis Rag.